# Fear Not the Night

# Fear Not the Night

### Based on the Classic Spirituality of
## *John* of the *Cross*
#### JOHN KIRVAN

**AVE MARIA PRESS**  Notre Dame, Indiana 46556

*John Kirvan* is the editor and author of several books including *The Restless Believers* and currently lives in Southern California where he writes primarily about classical spirituality.

For this work, early translations of various writings of St. John of the Cross, primarily parts of *The Ascent of Mount Carmel,* have been distilled and freely adapted into modern English and combined, rearranged, and paraphrased into a meditational format.

© 1998 Quest Associates.

International Standard Book Number: 0-87793-637-4

Library of Congress Catalog Card Number: 97-41440

Cover and text design by Elizabeth J. French.

Printed and bound in the United States of America.

# *Contents*

Though I suffer darkness
In this mortal life
That is not so hard a thing;
For though I have no light
I have the life of heaven.
For the blinder love is
The more it gives such life,
Holding the soul surrendered,
Living without light, in darkness.

—John of the Cross

# John of the Cross

John of the Cross's reputation so precedes him that it is hard not to be intimidated into turning back before ever making his spiritual acquaintance.

He is, after all, by common consent, the western spiritual master *par excellence*. He leads the seeking soul more deeply, more insistently, more uncompromisingly, and more sure-footedly into the mysteries of personal union with God than any other. Even for those who have never read a word he has written, his name conjures up mysterious dark nights of the soul that can seem to the easily dissuaded beginner more terrifying than inviting. His writings, as a result, are thought by many to be only for those who are far along the spiritual path and hardly suitable, or even accessible, to those taking their first well-meaning but stumbling spiritual steps.

But we must begin somewhere, and who could be a more trustworthy guide than someone who has arrived where we wish to go and who has mapped the soul's most direct route to the heart of its Creator. We can be sure that John's path is not one smoothed for dilettantes, but one carefully drawn to warn us of every tempting by-path, one that makes sure that we are never in doubt as to where we are going—final complete union with God— and what it takes to reach our destination. At the moment of our setting out and at every step along the way, St. John will make sure that we know that our spiritual baggage, however comfortable, however familiar and reassuring, everything that is not God, will have to be left behind.

The things we have most come to depend on, all those things with which we have filled our spiritual hope chest, our memories, our images, our accustomed words, will become by the light of John of the Cross not resources but hindrances to our growth, things to be abandoned so that God can fill our lives with himself. He will insist that we can get nowhere until we die to what we have always considered as life.

John's message is all about turning day into night. It is what we have to look forward to. It will not happen all at once, but by facing up to these great spiritual truths early in our journey we will begin to see our life in a quite different manner, and gain the most fundamental insight into the way of the Spirit. We will proceed without illusions—except, of course, those we insist on clinging to, and there will be, we can be sure, knowing ourselves as we do, many of these.

It is tempting to believe that this man who is one of Spain's greatest poets, who wrote several of the most important and theo-logically profound works of western spirituality, did so from a quiet monastic cell or a silent university library. In fact, he wrote his greatest poetry in a jail cell, and he spent most of his monastic life traveling thousands of miles back and forth across Spain, as he was involved in the nitty-gritty business and messy politics of helping Teresa of Avila reform the Carmelite order. At the same time he was a spiritual director who carried out his mission both in person and through correspondence. If all of this sounds dramatic, it wasn't. It was the same bone-tiring, day-by-day effort that is all too familiar to us.

This greatest of mystics found union with God in the tiring details and demands of everyday living. There is, after all, no other place to find God than where we find ourselves. And this applies to great saints such as John of the Cross as well as stumbling beginners like us.

# *How to Pray This Book*

The purpose of this book is to open a gate for you into the spiritual insight and wisdom of St. John of the Cross, considered by many to be western Christianity's supreme mystical theologian and one of Spain's most important poets.

This is not a book for mere reading. It invites you to meditate and pray its words on a daily basis over a period of thirty days and in a special way to enter into prayer through the unique doorway of St. John's extraordinary work, *The Ascent of Mount Carmel.* While this is a work written for those far advanced in the spiritual life, it is filled with guidance for those of us who are still at the foot of the mountain.

It is a handbook for a special kind of spiritual journey.

Before you read the "rules" for taking this journey, remember that this book is meant to free your spirit, not confine it. If on any day the meditation does not resonate well for you, turn elsewhere to find a passage which seems to best fit the spirit of your day and your soul. Don't hesitate to repeat a day as often as you like until you feel that you have discovered what the Spirit, through the words of the author, has to say to your spirit.

To help you along the way, here are some suggestions on one way to use this book as a cornerstone of your daily prayers. Each day employs the three forms of prayer central to western spiritual tradition: the lesson, the meditation, and the petition. The author of the classic *Cloud of Unknowing* has written that "they might better be called reading, reflecting, and praying. These three are so linked together that there can be no profitable reflection without first reading or hearing. Nor will beginners or even the spiritually adept come to true prayer without first taking time to reflect on what they have heard or read."

So for these thirty days there are daily readings developed from the writings of St. John. There follows a meditation in the form of a mantra to carry with you for reflection throughout the day. And there is an exercise for bringing your day to an end that asks you to find a place of quiet dark where you might enter into silence and a final, day's-end petitionary prayer.

But the forms and suggestions are not meant to become a straitjacket. Go where the Spirit leads you.

## *As Your Day Begins*

As the day begins, set aside a quiet moment in a quiet place to do the reading provided for the day.

The passages are short. They never run more than a couple of hundred words, but they have been carefully selected to give a spiritual focus, a spiritual center to your whole day. They are designed to remind you as another day begins of your own existence at a spiritual level. They are meant to put you in the presence of the spiritual master who is your companion and teacher on this journey.

Do not be discouraged, however, if you do not fully understand the reading. John of the Cross is a profound writer who does not release his wisdom at first glance. Don't be surprised if you understand very little the first time around. We have worked hard to provide easier access to his original text, but the words of the great mystics, like John of the Cross, can be pondered for a lifetime without their surrendering all their riches. Understanding is not the point. Your heart's response is. It may take time, perhaps a long time, for you to become comfortable with him. But in this thirty-day program you will be invited to do only what you can, to experience the Spirit in your own time and at your own pace. The effort required may prove to be difficult, but it could also be an unusually rewarding spiritual experience.

A word of advice: proceed slowly. Very slowly. The passages have been broken down into sense lines to help you do just this. Don't read to get to the end, but to savor each word, each phrase, each image. There is no predicting, no determining in advance what short phrase, what word will trigger a response in your spirit.

Give God a chance. After all, you are not reading these passages, you are praying them. You are establishing a mood of spiritual attentiveness for your whole day. What's the rush?

## *All Through Your Day*

Immediately following the day's reading you will find a single sentence, a meditation in the form of a mantra, a word borrowed from the Hindu tradition. This phrase is meant as a companion for your spirit as it moves through a busy day. Write it down on a 3" x 5" card or on the appropriate page of your daybook. Look at it as often as you can. Repeat it quietly to yourself, and go on your way.

It is not meant to stop you in your tracks or to distract you from responsibilities, but simply, gently, to remind you of the presence of God and your desire to respond to this presence.

You might consider carrying this mantric text from the day's reading with you in order to let its possible meaning sink more deeply into your imagination. Resist the urge to pull it apart, to make clean, clear, rational sense of it. A mantra is not an idea. It is a way of knowing God in a manner that emphasizes that the object of our search is immeasurably mysterious.

## *As Your Day Is Ending*

This is a time for letting go of the day, for entering a world of imaginative prayer.

We suggest that you choose a quiet, dark place that you can return to each day at its ending. When you come to it your first task is to quiet your spirit. Sit, or perhaps you are more comfortable kneeling. Do whatever stills your soul. Breath deeply. Inhale, exhale—slowly and deliberately, again and again until you feel your body let go of its tension.

This final prayer of the day is an act of trust and confidence, an entryway into peaceful sleep, a simple evening prayer that gathers together the spiritual character of the day that is now ending as it began—in the presence of God.

It is a time for summary and closure.

Invite God to embrace you with love and to protect you through the night.

Sleep well.

## Some Other Ways to Use This Book

1. Use it any way your spirit suggests. As mentioned earlier, skip a passage that doesn't resonate for you on a given day, or repeat for a second day or even several days a passage whose

richness speaks to you. The truths of a spiritual life are not absorbed in a day, or for that matter, in a lifetime. So take your time. Be patient with the Lord. Be patient with yourself.

2. Take two passages and/or their mantras—the more contrasting the better—and "bang" them together. Spend time discovering how their similarities or differences illumine your path.

3. Start a spiritual journal to record and deepen your experience of this thirty-day journey. Using either the mantra or another phrase from the reading that appeals to you, write a spiritual account of your day, a spiritual reflection. Create your own meditation.

4. Join millions who are seeking to deepen their spiritual life by joining with others to form a small group. More and more people

are doing just this to support each other in their mutual quest. Meet once a week, or at least every other week, to discuss and pray about one of the meditations.

# *Thirty Days with*
# *John of the Cross*

# Day One

## My Day Begins

The night of the soul
begins at that moment
when we look around
and see that all the creatures of heaven and earth
to which we are so firmly attached
are nothing compared to God.
"I looked at the earth,"
said Jeremiah, "and saw nothing.
I looked at the heavens, and I saw no light there."

We know at that moment
that our attachments to these things
are attachments to what is less than nothing.
They impede our reaching out to God,
and our transformation in him.

We know that we will never
comprehend the truth
as long as we depend on our own lights,
that we will never comprehend God,
as long as we are attached
to his creatures.
Their beauty
compared to the beauty of God
is ugliness.

Their grace and elegance
compared with God's grace
is crude.
Their goodness
measured by the goodness of God
seems hardly good at all.

We know that as long as we are
ensnared by our attachments to creatures
we will be incapable of union with God.

Until we are purged of these attachments,
we are not in a position
to possess God—
neither in this life or the next.
Thus does the night of the soul begin.

*All Through the Day*

Look again. . . .

## *My Day Is Ending*

As this night descends
remind me again that
the soul
that walks in love
neither rests
nor grows tired.

Let me look around
in the darkness
and see that all the creatures of heaven and earth
to which I am so firmly attached
are nothing compared to you.
Let me look at the earth

and at the heavens
with the eyes of Jeremiah
and see that there is no light there.
Let me come to know
here in the darkness
that my clutching at things
leaves me holding
what is less than nothing.

Descend on my soul now
like a river of peace
to take away my uncertainties,
my fear of the dark.

# *Day Two*

◆◆◆◆◆

## *My Day Begins*

As a beginner on the spiritual path
you will be tempted
to feel so privileged and enthusiastic
in your newfound devotion
that a kind of pride
may begin to manifest itself in your life.

And even though
living a good life
should engender humility,

you will begin to feel complacent,
even superior to your fellow travelers.
We will find you talking "spiritually,"
anxious to instruct others
despite the fact that you yourself
have taken only
the first stumbling steps
on the path to God.

Beware lest you condescend to others
who do not live up to your standards.
We are reminded of the publican
who boasted
that he was not like other men.
Do not become one of those complacent beginners

who in their spiritual presumption
publicly condemn others,
becoming more concerned
with the mote in their sister's eye
than the beam in their own.
They are blind guides
"who strain out a gnat,
and swallow a camel."

## *All Through the Day*

Beware the beam in your eye.

## *My Day Is Ending*

As this night descends
remind me again
that the soul
that walks in love
neither rests
nor grows tired.

I have taken
only the first stumbling steps
on the path to you my God,
but already I feel the temptation
to be like the publican
who boasted

that he was not like other men,
one of those complacent beginners
who in their spiritual presumption
become more concerned
with the mote in their sister's eye
than the beam in their own.

Descend on my soul now
like a river of peace
to take away my uncertainties,
my fear of the dark.

# *Day Three*

◆◆◆◆

## *My Day Begins*

When we take pride in our wisdom
we become, as St. Paul warns, "fools."
For all the world's wisdom
and all our skills
contrasted with the wisdom of God
are utter ignorance.

So if we count on our own wisdom
to bring about union with God,
we are truly ignorant
and will never reach our goal.

In our ignorance
we cannot know what true wisdom is.
Only those
who set aside their own knowledge
and walk in God's service
like unlearned children
receive wisdom from God.
"If anyone among you
thinks he is wise,
let him become ignorant
so as to be wise,
for the wisdom of this world
is foolishness with God."

Accordingly,

if we are to enter into God's wisdom
we will do it
by unknowing,
rather than by knowing.

What we consider light
must become darkness.

It is the night of our own
treasured wisdom.

*All Through the Day*

Let go of what you know.

# *My Day Is Ending*

As this night descends
remind me again
that the soul
that walks in love
neither rests
nor grows tired.

Hear the prayer of this fool
who takes pride in what I mistake for wisdom.
Help me to set aside my own knowledge
and walk in your service
like an untutored child.
Let me become ignorant

so as to be wise,
"for the wisdom of this world
is foolishness with God."

If I am to enter into your wisdom
I will do it
by unknowing,
rather than by knowing.
What I consider light
must become darkness.

Descend on my soul now
like a river of peace
to take away my uncertainties,
my fear of the dark.

# *Day Four*

◆◆◆◆

## *My Day Begins*

God is speaking to us
in the book of Proverbs when Solomon says:
"Simple ones, learn prudence;
foolish ones, pay attention.
Riches and honor, enduring wealth and prosperity
is with me.
My fruit is better than gold, even fine gold,
and my yield is better than choice silver."

We are the simple ones, the foolish ones.
He is speaking to those of us
who still cling to the things of this world.
We are the little ones,
because we are diminished
by the trivial things we treasure.
The riches and the glory we seek
are with him,
not where we have been looking.
We may think we know what is valuable,
but true riches
are to be found only in him,
and they are
more precious than gold or precious stones.
And the life he generates in our souls

is more precious than cherished silver,
more fruitful than any possible affection
we might have
for the things of this world.

All the wealth and glory of creation
is utter poverty and misery
in the Lord's sight.
The person who treasures them
is poor and miserable, too,
living so far
from the supreme riches and glory
that alone can satisfy the soul.
But it is not easy to let go.

## *All Through the Day*

We are what we love.

# My Day Is Ending

As this night descends
remind me again that
the soul
that walks in love
neither rests
nor grows tired.

I have been looking
in all the wrong places
for what is truly valuable,
for what can be found only in you.

I am one of the foolish ones
who still clings

to the things of this world,
diminished by the trivial things I treasure.
I have chosen utter poverty and misery
rather than the supreme riches and glory
that you alone can provide.
You alone can satisfy my soul.

And although I shall travel by night
and see only by the light of faith,
descend on my soul now
like a river of peace
to take away my uncertainties,
my fear of the dark.

# Day Five

## My Day Begins

If we only knew
how much spiritual good and abundance we lose
by not attempting to raise our desires
above childish things.
And if we only knew
to what extent,
by giving up our taste for trifles,
we might discover in simple spiritual food
our deepest satisfaction.

We are foolish and ignorant
if we think it is possible
to achieve union with God
without first emptying our lives
of all passions
for natural and even supernatural things
that can impede our union with God.
The difference between
what we desire
and the total transformation in God
that is offered to us
is enormous.

"Whoever of you does not renounce
all that he has
cannot be my disciple."

Be clear about this.
The son of man came
to teach a doctrine of letting go
of everything
that stands between us
and our Father.
Otherwise we cannot receive the gift
of his Spirit.
For as long as any one of us fails
to rid ourselves of our possessions,
we are incapable of receiving this Spirit
and the transformation
it works in us.

## *All Through the Day*

Let go of what you have.

## *My Day Is Ending*

As this night descends
remind me again that
the soul
that walks in love
neither rests
nor grows tired.

I know that it is foolish and ignorant
to think that I can achieve union with you
without first emptying my life
of all my trivial passions.
But I seem forever content
to restrict my soul

to childish things,
unaware, it seems,
of how much spiritual good and abundance
I so easily pass up,
blinding myself to the difference between
what I am content with
and the total transformation
that you have offered to me.

Descend on my soul now
like a river of peace
to take away my uncertainties,
my fear of the dark.

# *Day Six*

◆◆◆◆◆

## *My Day Begins*

When God ordered Moses
to climb to the top of the mountain
so that they might talk together,
he commanded him
to bring nothing with him,
to leave everything and everyone behind,
even the grazing cattle.
He was insisting
that the purpose of the journey upward

was to be alone with him,
with no distractions,
no other passions.

Much the same thing took place
when Jacob planned to climb Mount Bethel
to build an altar of sacrifice.
God insisted that before he started the climb
his people destroy all false gods,
purify themselves,
and put on new unsoiled clothes.

Our own ascent to God
makes the same demands on us:
a constant, ongoing effort
to renounce and mortify our passions.

The sooner we accomplish this,
the sooner we will reach the top,
the sooner we will talk with God.
But until our passions are eliminated
we will not arrive at the top,
no matter how much virtue we practice.
For we will fail to acquire perfect virtue
which requires
that before making a final ascent
into union with God
and the transformation that awaits us,
our souls must be emptied,
stripped, and purified
of all our other passions.

*All Through the Day*

Leave everything behind.

## *My Day Is Ending*

As this night descends
remind me again
that the soul
that walks in love
neither rests
nor grows tired.

But if I am to make this journey
to meet with you,
to talk with you,
to join with you,
I must, like Moses,
bring nothing with me.

I must leave everything behind.

Let me not forget
that the purpose of my journey
is to be alone with you,
with no distractions,
no other passion
but my desire to be with you.

Descend on my soul now
like a river of peace
to take away my uncertainties,
my fear of the dark.

# *Day Seven*

### *My Day Begins*

Our passions
drain our energy,
leaving us too tired
for the spiritual journey.

They are like small unreasonable children,
demanding,
impossible to please,
constantly whining
for this or that.

Above all they are never satisfied.

We find ourselves
forever weary from the effort
of searching for treasure
that is never enough,
and of digging wells
that are dry.

We are left
not only weak and empty,
more thirsty than when we began,
but upset and disturbed.
We are unable to find peace
or rest in anything.

Our passions are like

fires that blaze up when stoked by new fuel.
They rapidly consume it
and demand to be refueled
again and again.
But unlike a fire
that fades as its fuel is consumed
our passions become more intense.

Our hunger grows
the more it is fed.

And we grow weary.

## *All Through the Day*

Lest we grow too weary. . . .

# *My Day Is Ending*

As this night descends
remind me again
that the soul
that walks in love
neither rests
nor grows tired.

But I confess that I am
weary from the effort
of searching for treasure
that is never enough,
and of digging wells that are dry.

I am left
not only weak and empty,

more thirsty than when I began,
but upset and disturbed.
I am unable to find peace or rest
in anything.
Only you can slake my thirst
and satisfy my hunger.

Descend on my soul now
like a river of peace
to take away my uncertainties,
my fear of the dark.

# Day Eight

## *My Day Begins*

Anyone who allows their passions
to take charge of their life
finds themselves
tortured and afflicted
at the hands of a powerful captor.

Think of Samson,
once a symbol of great strength,
but in the hands of his enemies
he is weakened, blinded,

tortured, and tormented.
Our enemy is our passions.
We can expect the same.
The greater the number of our passions,
the greater is our torment.
"They surrounded me like bees," said David,
"they blazed like a fire of thorns."

"I go about mourning," he says.
"For my loins are filled with burning,
and there is no soundness in my flesh.
I am utterly spent and crushed;
I groan because of the tumult in my heart."
But while our passions torment us,
the Spirit of God refreshes us.

"Come to me all of you
who labor and are burdened," God says.
All you who go about
tormented and tortured,
all you who are weighed down
by your passions,
leave your captors behind
and come to me.
I will refresh you.
And you will find rest
for your souls.

*All Through the Day*

Come to me.

# *My Day Is Ending*

As this night descends
remind me again
that the soul
that walks in love
neither rests
nor grows tired.

"Come to me all of you
who labor and are burdened," God says.
I am one of those
who go about
tormented and tortured,
weighed down by my passions.

It is time for me
to leave my captors behind
and come to you.
Refresh my spirit
and give me rest, I pray.

Descend on my soul now
like a river of peace
to take away my uncertainties,
my fear of the dark.

# *Day Nine*

◆◆◆◆◆

## *My Day Begins*

Passion surrendered to
blinds our souls
because passion itself is blind.

We become like moths
dazzled by light
flying headlong to our destruction.

Passion is a strong light.
When stared into

it blinds us to the light beyond.
That light is so strong within us
that it darkens our intellect.

Passion is like dust in the eye of our souls;
until it is removed
we cannot see.

"If a blind man leads a blind man,
both will fall into the ditch."
We live unaware
of the spiritual light
to which we are willingly blind,
unaware of the evils
which each day
our passions visit upon us.

We convince ourselves
that with our intellect alone
we can avoid
the traps that passion sets before us,
and that total blindness
will never overtake our souls.

But we prefer
to grope our way through life
stumbling along,
walking in darkness,
when light is all around us.

*All Through the Day*

We stumble in the dark
when light is all around us.

## *My Day Is Ending*

As this night descends
remind me again
that the soul
that walks in love
neither rests
nor grows tired.

I have almost convinced myself
that with my intellect alone
I can avoid the traps
that passion sets before me,
and that total blindness
will never overtake my soul.

But I grope my way through life
stumbling along,
walking in the light of a false day,
when true light is around every corner.

Descend on my soul now
like a river of peace
to take away my uncertainties,
my fear of the dark.

# *Day Ten*

---

## *My Day Begins*

Passion is a thief.
Not only does it bring nothing to our lives,
but it robs us of whatever good
we already possess.

And if we do not bring it under control,
it will eat us alive.
It will kill off our relationship with God.
In the end it will be the only thing
that lives in our souls.

If we do not kill it first,
it will kill us.

When we allow passion
to distract us from God
the attempt to practice virtue
becomes a sad burden.
We live dissatisfied
with ourselves,
unfeeling
toward our neighbors,
lazy
in our relationship with God.
Sapped of spiritual strength,
we are ill.

We are, in truth, dying—
tormented, weary,
weak, and blind.

On the other hand,
if we overturn passion's grip on us,
by turning our lives
with single-mindedness to God,
then peace will flower in us
with newfound strength,
renewed energy,
and restored sight.

## *All Through the Day*

Restore what is mine.

# *My Day Is Ending*

As this night descends
remind me again
that the soul
that walks in love
neither rests
nor grows tired.

But when my steps
are driven by passion,
my every attempt to practice virtue
becomes a sad burden.
I am, in truth, dying—
tormented, weary,
weak, and blind.

Overturn, I pray, passion's hold on me.
Turn my life back to you
with single-mindedness.
Renew my strength and energy.
Restore my sight.

Descend on my soul now
like a river of peace
to take away my uncertainties,
my fear of the dark.

# *Day Eleven*

◆◆◆◆

## *My Day Begins*

Unless our souls are on fire
with a longing for spiritual things,
a longing more urgent than our passions,
we will never be able
to overcome the pull of nature,
never escape
the imprisonment of our souls
by passions long indulged.

We resist entering
the night of the senses.
It will take all our courage
to live in the darkness of a life
willingly emptied
of passing satisfactions,
a life where once cultivated passions
are now discarded.

Only a greater love
can replace a love we have cherished.
If we wish, therefore,
to overcome the passions of life
and deny pleasure's power over us,
we can do it only

by kindling another, better love.

Only by finding our satisfaction and strength
in this better love
will we have the courage and constancy
to deny all other passions.

Only then
will our houses be stilled,
our desires laid to rest,
our passions no longer at war
with our spirits.

Only then
will we walk in freedom,
enjoying union with our God.

## *All Through the Day*

A better love is needed.

# My Day Is Ending

As this night descends
remind me again that
the soul
that walks in love
neither rests
nor grows tired.

Here in this darkness
let me taste a love great enough
to replace all the loves I have cherished,
for only then can I
overcome their power over me.
Kindle in me that other, better love

which alone
can bring to me
satisfaction and strength,
courage and constancy.
Only then will my house be stilled,
my desires laid to rest,
my passions no longer at war
with my spirit.
Only then will I walk in freedom.

Descend on my soul now
like a river of peace
to take away my uncertainties,
my fear of the dark.

# *Day Twelve*

◆◆◆◆◆

## *My Day Begins*

All of us bear
some small resemblance to God.
We are, after all, made in God's image and likeness.
But we are separated by an infinite difference.
We cannot, however great our desire,
however graced,
come to know God
in the way that we know
any other person, any other thing.

Our senses,
through which all our other knowledge comes,
cannot convey
a clear knowledge of God
to our souls.

"No one shall see me," Moses was told,
"and remain alive."

John says:
"No one has ever seen God,
or anything like him."

"To what have you been able
to liken God?

Or what image
will you fashion like unto him?"
Isaiah says.

Our failure
is not a failure of mere reverence
in the face of the divine.
It is a question
of a difference
that cannot be erased
by what our minds can understand,
our wills effect,
our imaginations create.
Faith alone
bridges the difference.

## *All Through the Day*

My eyes do not see,
nor do my ears hear.

# My Day Is Ending

As this night descends
remind me again that
the soul
that walks in love
neither rests
nor grows tired.

Remind me too
that the distance between us
is not a failure to be overcome
by effort.
It is a difference
that cannot be erased

by what my mind can understand,
my will effect,
or my imagination create.
Faith alone
can bridge the difference.

It will always be night.
No one has ever seen you,
or anything like you.

Descend on my soul now
like a river of peace
to take away my uncertainties,
my fear of the dark.

# Day Thirteen

◆◆◆◆

## *My Day Begins*

Our spiritual ascent
is a journey by night.
Faith is our only light
in the hours after midnight,
when all we have come to depend on
can no longer point the way.

We move toward God
not by understanding,
not by drawing on and relying on

what we know from experience
gained in the clear light of day,
not by what we feel or can imagine,
but by belief . . . by faith.

For God's being
exceeds the grasp of our intellect,
our imagination, and all our faculties.
Indeed it cannot be known in this life.
Our best efforts are not enough.
They leave us infinitely distant from God,
from union with him.

"No eye has seen.
nor ear heard,
nor heart conceived

what God has prepared
for those who love him."

Therefore as long as we cling
to what we can understand,
imagine, or even desire,
especially as long as we depend
on our own efforts,
we will not reach
a goal that transcends all that we are,
all that we can achieve.
We must move
from knowing to unknowing,
from daylight to the night of faith.

*All Through the Day*

We journey by night.

## *My Day Is Ending*

As this night descends
remind me again that
the soul
that walks in love
neither rests
nor grows tired.

Remind me too that as long as I cling
to what I can understand,
imagine, or even desire,
especially as long as I depend
on my own efforts,
I will never enter into a life

that transcends all that I am,
all that I can achieve
through my own efforts.

It is time
to move from knowing to unknowing,
from daylight to the night of faith.

Descend on my soul now
like a river of peace
to take away my uncertainties,
my fear of the dark.

# *Day Fourteen*

◆◆◆◆◆

## *My Day Begins*

"Faith is the assurance
of things hoped for,
the certitude
of things not seen."

Therefore if we
"would draw near to God we must believe."

Only by means of faith,
only, that is, when we approach God

in divine light,
exceeding all understanding,
does he manifest himself to our souls.

To see God is not to know,
but to believe.
Nothing else will do.
The deeper our faith,
the closer is our union with God.

Therefore we must begin our ascent to God
with minds and souls
emptied of whatever images,
whatever ideas of him,
have come through our senses.

We must make our ascent in faith
blindly,
content with darkness.
For the God we seek
is wrapped in obscurity,
"He has made darkness
and the dark water
his dwelling place."

God approaches in blinding light
that is darkness to our eyes.
In the same darkness
we make our ascent.

## *All Through the Day*

We make our ascent in darkness.

# *My Day Is Ending*

As this night descends
remind me again that
the soul
that walks in love
neither rests
nor grows tired.

You approach me
in a blinding light
that is darkness to my eyes.
You have made darkness
and the dark water
your dwelling place.

But it is in this darkness
and only here
that I must approach you
and make my ascent
into the union I so much desire.

To approach you is not to know,
but to believe.
Nothing else will do.

Descend on my soul now
like a river of peace
to take away my uncertainties,
my fear of the dark.

# Day Fifteen

## My Day Begins

If faith is light to our souls
permitting us to see the unseeable,
then why do we call it
a midnight kind of darkness?

It is darkness
in the same way
that any blinding light
is a kind of darkness.

The overwhelming light of faith
eclipses our intellect
and what it can see.

The light of faith
is like the light of the sun,
so bright that when it is shining
all other lights
seem not to be lights at all,
all other ways of seeing
seem not to be seeing.

The light of faith
does not improve our human sight,
it overwhelms it.

Discovering the light of faith
is like being born blind
and then being introduced to colors
we have never seen.
It is seeing with a wholly
new kind of sight.

When we see with the eyes of faith,
we are seeing in the dark.

*All Through the Day*

We see in the dark.

# My Day Is Ending

As this night descends
remind me again that
the soul
that walks in love
neither rests
nor grows tired.

In the darkness of this night
restore my soul.
Let me see
by the light of faith,
for all other ways of seeing
seem not to be seeing at all.

I was born blind,
now I see colors
I never knew existed.

I am seeing
with a wholly new kind of sight.

I am seeing in the dark.

Descend on my soul now
like a river of peace
to take away my uncertainties,
my fear of the dark.

# *Day Sixteen*

◆◆◆◆◆

## *My Day Begins*

Too often
we become so preoccupied
with the rind of the orange
that we never get to the fruit.

I mean we become so fascinated,
so satisfied
with our private store of images of God
that we never get to God himself.
He cannot break through our distraction,
through the surface of our prayers.

Our ideas about God
are like curtains that veil
the spiritual riches
that lie behind them.

Since God
cannot be captured in any single image,
in any specific idea,
we must put our temptation
to define God behind us
in order to be united with God.

"The Lord said to Moses:
'Gather the people to me . . .'
and they came near
and stood at the foot of the mountain

while the mountain burned with the fire of heaven.
Then the Lord spoke out of the midst of the fire.
They heard the sound of words,
but saw no form.
There was only a voice.

'Since you saw no form
when the Lord spoke to you at Horeb
out of the midst of the fire,
beware lest you act corruptly
by making a graven image for yourself.'"

*All Through the Day*

Beware of false gods.

# *My Day Is Ending*

As this night descends
remind me again that
the soul
that walks in love
neither rests
nor grows tired.

Let me enter this night
content to know
that I will never capture you
with my imagination.
Let me put behind me
every temptation to define you.

Help me to lose my fascination
with the rind of the orange,
my comfortable satisfaction
with my private store of images of you.

Otherwise I will never get to you,
never get beyond the curtains
my imagination weaves,
never taste the fruit of the matter.

Descend on my soul now
like a river of peace
to take away my uncertainties,
my fear of the dark.

# *Day Seventeen*

### *My Day Begins*

Our images of God,
even the most beautiful and powerful,
even the ones that prompt us to pray
and reach out in charity,
can sabotage our ascent to God.
The problem comes when we begin to think
that God is somewhat like these images.
In truth they are far from what God is like.

"We ought not to think that the nature of God
is anything like gold or silver or stone images,
shaped by human art and skill."

They are a starting point,
but when we rest in them,
when we become content with them,
they distract us from the one route,
the only route that allows us to ascend
to the union with God that is our goal.

They distract us from naked faith.
Think of your ascent to God
as mounting a staircase.
No matter how comfortable—
or weary—

you may feel,
no one of the steps should be mistaken
for the final step.
Your goal is the dark at the top of the stairs.
If in climbing
you don't keep leaving each step behind
because of your desire to stay on one of them,
you never advance.
You certainly never reach the top
and the peace it promises—
the peace that prompted you
to take your first step.

## *All Through the Day*

This is not the time to rest.

# *My Day Is Ending*

As this night descends
remind me again that
the soul
that walks in love
neither rests
nor grows tired.

But I am tired,
and a part of me
wants nothing more than to rest,
and find peace
where I am.

I need you to remind me

this night
that my goal is not here.
It is the dark at the top of the stairs.
Let me leave my weariness behind,
remembering why I am here
and what prompted me
to take my first step
toward you.

Descend on my soul now
like a river of peace
to take away my uncertainties,
my fear of the dark.

# *Day Eighteen*

◆◆◆◆◆

## *My Day Begins*

In your ascent to God
it is important to remember
that with each step of the journey
you not only leave something behind,
you enter into
a new and different relationship with God.
God does more,
you do less.
God refreshes you

with a deeper quiet, a more untroubled calm,
a more profound peace.

So it is sad
that when we are given the gift of peace
we try to retrace our steps
to a more comfortable spiritual world,
one we have grown used to,
but which we are meant to leave behind.

We have to learn how
to remain at rest
with quiet attention to God,
and ignore our desire
to keep busy.
The security of activity

must give way to the unknown,
to the darkness of faith.

There will be moments when
hard-earned patterns of prayer and meditation
will have to be let go of
so that the spirit can pray within us.

The more we fight this moment,
the more uncomfortable we will become.
Our attempts
to remain in control
will pull us ever farther from the peace
with which we have already been gifted.

*All Through the Day*

Stop struggling.

# My Day Is Ending

As this night descends
remind me again that
the soul
that walks in love
neither rests
nor grows tired.

In the quiet of this night,
if only for a moment,
let me stop struggling
to hold on to the comfort
of what I have,
of what I know,

of what I am at ease with.

I cannot remain in control,
for it will forever pull me farther
from the peace
that you have already given me.

I must let go
and let you do what only you can.

Descend on my soul now
like a river of peace
to take away my uncertainties,
my fear of the dark.

# Day Nineteen

### My Day Begins

Not every desire
to give up our tried and treasured
spiritual practices
comes from God.

It could be that
the difficulties we encounter in prayer
are not God prompting us to move on,
but our own laziness
prompting us to drag our feet.

A sure sign
that we have not outgrown our images of God
in favor of a purer, more spiritual prayer life
is that we would
rather think of anything else
but God.

The truest sign
that the Spirit is drawing us along,
that it is time to take the next step,
is that we have come
to appreciate being alone
in quiet, loving awareness
of God's presence,
without a need
to justify ourselves

by reviving familiar methods of prayer
and distracting ourselves with images
that might have served us well
but at this moment are not needed.
The more you become accustomed
to this more profound calmness of spirit,
the more your knowledge and love of God will grow.
Without crippling strain,
you will know a deeper peace,
a more lasting joy.

## *All Through the Day*

Time spent with God
needs no justification.

# *My Day Is Ending*

As this night descends
remind me again that
the soul
that walks in love
neither rests
nor grows tired.

It is not always easy
to come to this quiet time
and think only of you.
Sometimes I would rather
think of anything else
but you.

Laziness overtakes my soul.
I drag my feet.

Deepen my desire to be alone
in quiet, loving awareness of your presence,
without a need to console myself
with images and prayers
that once might have served me well
but that are no longer needed.

Descend on my soul now
like a river of peace
to take away my uncertainties,
my fear of the dark.

# *Day Twenty*

◆◆◆◆◆

## *My Day Begins*

There are moments when
it will seem to us
that prayer is beyond us
because we cannot summon up
the words and images
that have always been at our disposal.

There are any number of natural reasons for this.

But there comes a time
when the emptiness of our minds and souls
is a gift of God.
For as long as
our spirits are filled with a God
constructed from our images and words
there is no room for a God
who goes beyond all our words.

Be content,
however puzzled and uncomfortable you may be,
to remain in the presence of God,
lovingly attentive,
your mind so quiet,
so unoccupied,

that it will seem
that you are doing nothing,
that you are idling,
wasting your time.

Quieting our busy, distracted souls
is no small achievement,
no small gift.

"Be still
and know
that I am God."

## *All Through the Day*

Be still and know that God is here.

## *My Day Is Ending*

As this night descends
remind me again that
the soul
that walks in love
neither rests
nor grows tired.

And as the darkness of this night settles,
quiet my busy, distracted soul.
Let me be still and know
that you are God.
However content
or puzzled and uncomfortable I may be,

let me remain in your presence,
lovingly attentive,
my mind unoccupied.
I know that this is no easy thing,
no small achievement,
no small gift.

Descend on my soul now
like a river of peace
to take away my uncertainties,
my fear of the dark.

# *Day Twenty-One*

## *My Day Begins*

When God descended
into the temple
that Solomon had just completed,
he came in darkness.

The Lord has
set the sun in the heavens,
but has said
that he would dwell in thick darkness.

When God spoke to Moses
he wrapped himself in a cloud.

Gideon's troops
could not see the light of the lamps they carried
until the vessels that held them were broken.
Only then did the light blaze forth.

There is divine light within us,
but only when our mortal shell is broken
will we see its full splendor.
Until then God will communicate with us
wrapped in darkness
and the obscurity of faith.

It is a darkness
that will be dispelled

only when the darkness of faith
will no longer be necessary.
"Our knowledge is imperfect,
but when the perfect comes
the imperfect will pass away."

## *All Through the Day*

Our knowledge is imperfect.

# My Day Is Ending

As this night descends
remind me again
that the soul
that walks in love
neither rests
nor grows tired.
Yet it also walks in a darkness
that will be dispelled
only when the darkness of faith
will no longer be necessary.
Until the perfect comes
my knowledge of you will be imperfect.
Until then I will not see

the full splendor of your light
that I carry within me.
Until then you will communicate with me
wrapped in darkness
and the obscurity of faith.

Descend on my soul now
like a river of peace
to take away my uncertainties,
my fear of the dark.

# *Day Twenty-Two*

◆◆◆◆◆

## *My Day Begins*

Not only do we not have
to leave all the doors to our souls open
to allow God in,
the opposite is true.
We need to close and lock the doors
of our souls,
not only to passions and desires,
but to ideas and images of God,
and above all

to the storehouse of memories and imaginings
that we have collected over the years,
hoping to find in them
a path to God.

We have put our trust
in keeping open all the doors to our souls.
But we need to remember
the risen Jesus
passed through closed doors
to enter the room where his apostles waited
for the peace
that only he could bring.

In the same way
he enters our souls,

without our knowing how,
without any effort on our part;
but only if we shut and lock the doors of our souls
to our ideas of him,
our memories of experiences,
and all our imaginings.
Only then will he descend on our souls
like a river of peace
to take away our uncertainties,
our little upsets,
our fear of the dark.

*All Through the Day*

He enters through closed doors.

# *My Day Is Ending*

As this night descends
remind me again that
the soul
that walks in love
neither rests
nor grows tired.

Once you passed through closed doors
to enter the room where your apostles waited
for the peace
that only you could bring.

I too wait for you,
knowing that in the same way

you will enter my soul,
without my knowing how,
without any effort on my part,
once I have shut and locked the door of my soul
against all my expectations.

Descend on my soul now
like a river of peace
to take away my uncertainties,
my fear of the dark.

# *Day Twenty-Three*

◆◆◆◆◆

## *My Day Begins*

Nothing paralyzes the devil
more effectively
than closing the doors
of our souls
to the most fertile agents of evil:
our imagination and our memory.

Rather than the peace
that Christ brings,

the devil carries with him
the root sins
of pride, greed,
anger, envy, and lust—
using the faculties of our souls
as instruments of evil.

In a soul kept open to every memory
and welcoming to every imagining
it becomes difficult
to recognize the difference between
what our best soul has wrought
and what the devil has brought.

With memory and imagination
comes not just evil,

but sicknesses of the soul:
weariness, sadness,
moodiness,
and above all, constant distractions
from the one thing that matters—
our commitment to moving
beyond what we can understand
to a life with the God
who exceeds all our attempts
at understanding.

Keeping the doors
closed to memory and imagination
frees up our souls for the ascent we have begun.

## *All Through the Day*

Closed doors free the soul.

# My Day Is Ending

As this night descends
remind me again that
the soul
that walks in love
neither rests
nor grows tired.

But if I keep my soul open to every memory
and welcome every imagining,
in time I will not know the difference
between what my best soul has wrought
and what the devil has brought.

Overpower my distractions
that draw me away
from the one thing that matters—
my desire to move
beyond what I can understand
to a life with you
who exceed all my attempts
at understanding.

Descend on my soul now
like a river of peace
to take away my uncertainties,
my fear of the dark.

# *Day Twenty-Four*

◆◆◆◆◆

## *My Day Begins*

When we allow our memories
and our imagination
to clutter up our hearts
there is little or no room
left for God.

Until we learn how
to forget and put aside
the demands of our passions
and learn how to discipline our memory

and our imagination,
our hearts are destined
to be always in turmoil,
our souls never at peace.

But when we learn
how to forget,
there is nothing running loose in our lives
that can disturb us,
nothing to agitate our passions,
nothing to confuse our hearts.

After all,
our hearts are not attracted
to what they don't see.

Think about how your memories affect you.
Some produce fear and apprehension,
irritation or mere annoyance.
Others summon up joy
or rekindle desire.
None of them
leaves our hearts untouched,
our souls unmoved.

All of them
cloud our vision
of the God
to whom we wish to ascend.

## *All Through the Day*

Try not to remember.

# *My Day Is Ending*

As this night descends
remind me again that
the soul
that walks in love
neither rests
nor grows tired.

But until I learn how
to forget and put aside
the demands of my passions
and learn how to discipline my memory
and my imagination,
my heart is destined

to be always in turmoil,
my soul never at peace,
my heart cluttered
with little or no room
left for you, my God.

Uncloud my vision.

Descend on my soul now
like a river of peace
to take away my uncertainties,
my fear of the dark.

# Day Twenty-Five

◆◆◆◆◆

## *My Day Begins*

If everything were to go wrong for you,
if your whole world were to fall apart,
there would still be no point
in getting upset.

On the contrary,
confronting everything
that happens to us
with serenity
not only protects our peace of soul,

but carries with it
its own blessings.

For one thing,
it keeps our problems in perspective
and helps us
identify the right remedy.
We are not meant to live in misery,
but in joy.

Solomon said:
"God has made everything beautiful
in its time. . . .
There is nothing better for his people
than to be happy
and enjoy themselves

as long as they live. . . .
It is God's gift
that they should eat and drink
and take pleasure in all their toil."
Everything that happens,
good or bad,
should be an occasion to rejoice
rather than to be troubled.
But to remain serene,
our hearts
must be free
of everything but God.

## *All Through the Day*

God has made everything beautiful.

## *My Day Is Ending*

As this night descends
remind me again that
the soul
that walks in love
neither rests
nor grows tired.

Remind me again
that everything that happens,
good or bad,
should be an occasion to rejoice
rather than to be troubled.
But to remain serene

my heart must be free
of everything but you.

As this day ends,
let me look back on all that was good
and all that seemed bad
and see it as you have made it,
beautiful.

Descend on my soul now
like a river of peace
to take away my uncertainties,
my fear of the dark.

# *Day Twenty-Six*

### *My Day Begins*

At this stage of our lives
we are bound to God
through hope,
by our commitment to things not yet seen.
We hope for
that which we do not yet possess.

Therefore to be truly hopeful
we need to empty our souls
of all that is not God,

all those images and ideas of God
created by our imagination
and stored in our memory.

They give us a false security
that we already possess
what in truth is still
only an object of hope.
What we remember and imagine
is not God.
God is what we hope for.
Everything we hold on to
betrays our hope.

The more we shed our memories
and our treasured images of God,

the more we will come to rely on hope,
and the deeper our hope,
the stronger our union
with God will be.
We ascend to God through hope.
If we are honest with ourselves
we must admit
that it is difficult
to let go of the comfort and warmth
of what we think we know,
for a journey of naked hope.
But there is no other path.

## *All Through the Day*

We live in hope.

# *My Day Is Ending*

As this night descends
remind me again that
the soul
that walks in love
neither rests
nor grows tired.

Let me walk in hope,
without the false security
of thinking that I already possess
what is in truth
still only an object of hope.
What I remember and imagine is not you.

You are what I hope for.
Everything I hold on to
betrays my hope.

Help me to exchange the comfort and warmth
of what I think I know
for a journey of naked hope.
There is no other path.

Descend on my soul now
like a river of peace
to take away my uncertainties,
my fear of the dark.

# *Day Twenty-Seven*

## *My Day Begins*

Too often
our carefully cultivated and protected
spiritual experiences and insights
trigger pride and self-satisfaction
rather than humility.
We begin to think
that we are especially gifted by God,
and we get to feeling good about our gifts
and ourselves.

Like the gospel pharisee,
we begin to thank God
that we are not like other people.

Not only, we think, does the fact
that we enjoy beautiful images of God
and warm feelings of his presence
mean that we are closer to him,
but that those who do not enjoy these experiences
are far from him.

We need first of all
to understand that our closeness to God
is not measured
by our imaginative glimpses of him,
or any other "spiritual" experiences.

It is measured
by the depth of our humility,
by our disdain for our own self-worth,
and by our desire not to be seen as privileged,
but as worth nothing
compared to the God we seek.

In our ascent,
none of our experiences is worth
a single act of humility,
that seeks not itself
but the good of others.

*All Through the Day*

Walk humbly.

# *My Day Is Ending*

As this night descends
remind me again that
the soul
that walks in love
neither rests
nor grows tired.

But remind me also
that I must walk in humility.

My closeness to you
is not measured
by the beauty of my thoughts,
but by the depth of my humility,
by my disdain for my own self-importance.

I am nothing
compared to you.
None of my experiences is worth
a single act of humility,
that seeks not itself
but the good of others.

Descend on my soul now
like a river of peace
to take away my uncertainties,
my fear of the dark.

# Day Twenty-Eight

## *My Day Begins*

The great temptation of the persons,
places, and things in our lives
is to make them
the beginning and end of our joy.
But only by detaching ourselves from them
can we come to a joy in them
that does not block our ascent to God.

There is a world of difference
between the joy of someone
whose goal is
to possess and accumulate things
and the joy of the one who sees in things
something not to be surrendered to
but to be given away.

It is the difference
between seeing the true good
in persons, places, and things
and clinging to them
for what is worst in them.

True joy in things
leads to generosity.

False joy
ends in possessiveness
that in turn ends
in our being possessed.

By detaching ourselves from things
we possess them in liberty;
when we cling to them
we become
their captive.

The joy of creation
becomes no joy at all.

◆◆◆◆◆

*All Through the Day*

In truth there is joy.

◆◆◆◆◆

# My Day Is Ending

As this night descends
remind me again that
the soul
that walks in love
neither rests
nor grows tired.

Let me end this day
knowing the difference between
possessing and accumulating things
and the joy of someone who sees in things
something not to be surrendered to
but to be given away.

Let this day end with a generous heart,
not making the places and things of my life
the beginning and end of my joy.

And when this night has passed
let me waken to a world
where I see the true good
in persons, places, and things
and not cling
to what is worst in them.

Descend on my soul now
like a river of peace
to take away my uncertainties,
my fear of the dark.

# *Day Twenty-Nine*

## *My Day Begins*

We might wish it to be otherwise,
but "that which is born of the flesh
is flesh
and that which is born of the spirit
is spirit."

So we should not be surprised
that Jesus has said to us
that we must be born anew.

We should not fool ourselves
into believing that we can grow
in the life of the spirit
by catering
to the life of our senses.

Therefore:
"look not to the things that are seen,
but to the things that are unseen.
For the things that are seen
pass in a moment,
but the things that are unseen
last forever."
If you deny yourself
a passing joy of the senses

God will reward you
a hundredfold—
even in this life.
But the opposite is also true.
Surrender to your senses,
and sorrow and anguish
will be yours a hundredfold.

Until we triumph over our senses
we will never know
the calm serenity and peace,
the lasting joy
of life lived in God.

## *All Through the Day*

The unseen lasts forever.

# *My Day Is Ending*

As this night descends
remind me again that
the soul
that walks in love
neither rests
nor grows tired.

Don't let me fool myself
into believing that I can grow
in the life of the spirit
by catering
to the life of my senses.

May I be born anew
of the spirit
in the dark silence
of this night
and know
in all the coming days
the hundredfold reward of your love.

Descend on my soul now
like a river of peace
to take away my uncertainties,
my fear of the dark.

# *Day Thirty*

## *My Day Begins*

We would be very foolish
to think that God is letting us down
because we go without spiritual comfort,
or, on the other hand,
believe that we possess God
because we feel good.
We would be even more foolish
were we to use up our spiritual energies
pursuing such comfort
or being content with finding it.

When we think and act this way
we are no longer pursuing God.
We are chasing after things,
exalted things surely,
but still things,
still not God
whom we can pursue
only in unencumbered faith, hope, and charity.

To be content
with anything short of God
is to tie ourselves down,
our will unable to rise above itself.
We will never enjoy
the pure sweetness of union with God

as long as we are content
with the passing consolations of this life.

If we are to succeed
in our ascent
we must leave all appetites,
except the appetite for God,
unsatisfied.
We must empty our souls of everything
except a hunger
that only God can satisfy.

## *All Through the Day*

Be content to go hungry.

# *My Day Is Ending*

As this night descends
remind me again that
the soul
that walks in love
neither rests
nor grows tired.

But if I am to succeed
on this journey
I must leave all my appetites,
except the appetite for you, my God,
unsatisfied,
my soul empty of everything

but a hunger that only you
can satisfy.

I know I will never
enjoy the pure sweetness of union with you
as long as I am content
with the passing consolations of this life.
To be content
with anything short of you
would be to tie myself down,
unable to come to you.

Descend on my soul now
like a river of peace
to take away my uncertainties,
my fear of the dark.

# One Final Word

This thirty-day journey of the spirit is only the first step along a spiritual path laid out by one of history's great spiritual teachers. There is much more to the journey and certainly much more to the spiritual wisdom of John of the Cross.

You may have already decided that John of the Cross is someone whose experience of God is one that you wish to study more closely and deeply. In that case you should read more. There is no shortage of material by and about this extraordinary theologian and practitioner of the spiritual life. His own works, both scholarly treatises and poetry, fill several volumes.

You may, however, have decided that his writings are beyond you, just too intimidating at this point in your life, or simply not to your taste. After all, he wrote primarily for those very advanced in the spiritual life. Whatever your response to this basic introduction to John of the Cross, you may wish to remember a few lines he wrote in 1589 to someone who, lacking in spiritual consolations, apparently felt that the route God was taking her on was not what she expected. To her he wrote:

> What do you think serving God involves other than avoiding evil, keeping his commandments, and being occupied with the things of God as best we can? If you have this, there is no call for extraordinary graces. It is a great favor from God when he leaves you in the dark with nothing to guide you but unadorned faith and hope.

It is this grounding in common sense, underlying even the most esoteric of his writings, that makes his teaching so worthy of your trust. And it will remain a healthy reminder of what is in the end the basic truth of every spiritual journey, no matter in whose footsteps you choose to walk.

Never forget there are many other teachers. Somewhere there is the right teacher for your own, very special, absolutely unique journey of the spirit. You will find your teacher; you will discover your path.

We would not be searching, as St. Augustine reminds us, if we had not already found.

One more thing should be said.

Spirituality is not meant to be self-absorption, a cocoon-like relationship between God and self. In the long run, if it is to have meaning, if it is to grow and not wither, it must be a wellspring of compassionate living. It must reach out to others as God has reached out to us.

True spirituality breaks down the walls of our souls and lets in not just heaven, but the whole world.

February 25, 1997

**Other Titles in the *Thirty Days with a Great Spiritual Teacher* series:**

ALL WILL BE WELL
Based on the Classic Spirituality of *Julian of Norwich*

◆

GOD AWAITS YOU
Based on the Classic Spirituality of *Meister Eckhart*

◆

LET NOTHING DISTURB YOU
A Journey to the Center of the Soul with *Teresa of Avila*

◆

LET THERE BE LIGHT
Based on the Visionary Spirituality of *Hildegard of Bingen*

◆

LIVING IN THE PRESENCE OF GOD
The Everyday Spirituality of *Brother Lawrence*

◆

PEACE OF HEART
Based on the Life and Teachings of *Francis of Assisi*

SET ASIDE EVERY FEAR
Love and Trust in the Spirituality of *Catherine of Siena*

◆

SET YOUR HEART FREE
The Practical Spirituality of *Francis de Sales*

◆

SIMPLY SURRENDER
Based on the Little Way of *Thérèse of Lisieux*

◆

THAT YOU MAY HAVE LIFE
Let the Mystics Be Your Guide for Lent

◆

TRUE SERENITY
Based on Thomas á Kempis' *The Imitation of Christ*

◆

WHERE ONLY LOVE CAN GO
A Journey of the Soul into *The Cloud of Unknowing*

◆

YOU SHALL NOT WANT
A Spiritual Journey Based on *The Psalms*